A QUESTRON™ ELECTRONIC WORKBOOK

MY FIRST BOOK OF ADDITION

PRICE/STERN/SLOAN
Publishers, Inc., Los Angeles
DISTRIBUTED BY
RANDOM HOUSE, INC.
New York

THE QUESTRON™ SYSTEM
COMBINING FUN WITH LEARNING

This book is part of **THE QUESTRON SYSTEM**, which offers children a unique aid to learning and endless hours of challenging entertainment.

The QUESTRON electronic "wand" uses a microchip to sense correct and incorrect answers with "right" or "wrong" sounds and lights. Victory sounds and lights reward the user when particular sets of questions or games are completed. Powered by a nine-volt alkaline battery, which is activated only when the wand is pressed on a page, QUESTRON should have an exceptionally long life. The QUESTRON ELECTRONIC WAND can be used with any book in the QUESTRON series.

A note to parents...

With QUESTRON, right or wrong answers are indicated instantly and can be tried over and over to reinforce learning and improve skills. Children need not be restricted to the books designated for their age group, as interests and rates of development vary widely. Also, within many of the books, certain pages are designed for the older end of the age group and will provide a stimulating challenge to younger children.

Many activities are designed at different levels. For example, the child can select an answer by recognizing a letter or by reading an entire word. The activities for pre-readers and early readers are intended to be used with parental assistance. Interaction with parents or older children will stimulate the learning experience.

QUESTRON Project Director: Roger Burrows
Educational Consultants: Susan Parker, Rozanne Lanczak
Writer: Beverley Dietz
Illustrator: Susan Nethery
Graphic Designers: Judy Walker, Lee A. Scott

 Published by Price/Stern/Sloan Publishers, Inc., 410 North La Cienega Boulevard, Los Angeles, California 90048. Distributed by Random House, Inc., 201 East 50th Street, New York, New York 10022. ISBN: 0-394-87705-5

1 2 3 4 5 6 7 8 9 0

Printed in the United States of America

HOW TO START **QUESTRON**

Hold **QUESTRON**
at this angle and
press the activator button
firmly on the page.

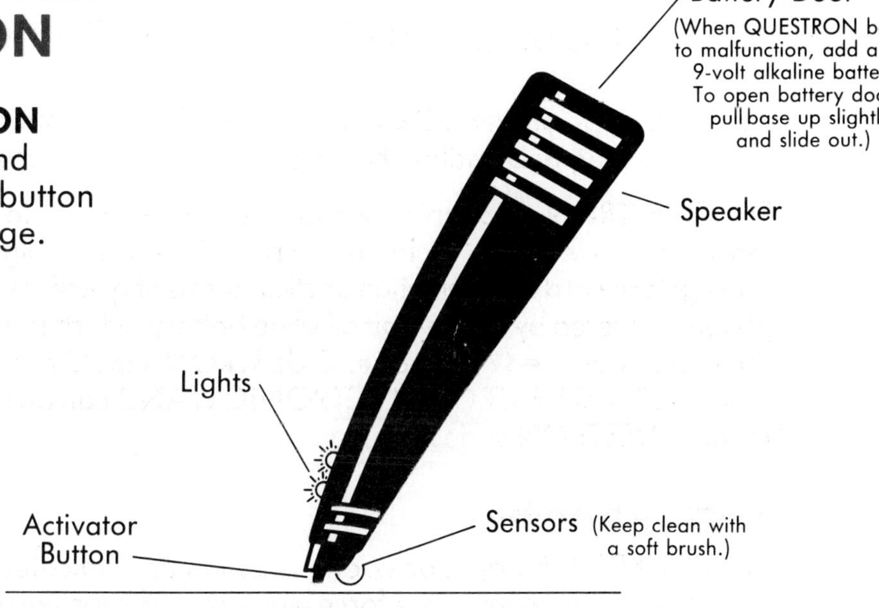

HOW TO USE **QUESTRON**

PRESS
Press **QUESTRON** firmly
on the shape below,
then lift it off.

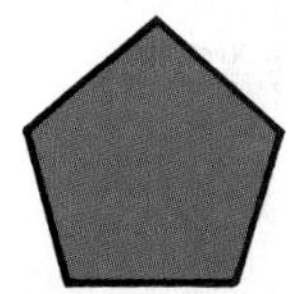

TRACK
Press **QUESTRON** down on "Start"
and keep it pressed down
as you move to "Finish."

RIGHT & WRONG WITH **QUESTRON**

Press **QUESTRON**
on the square.

See the green light and
hear the sound. This
green light and sound
say "You are correct."

Press **QUESTRON**
on the circle.

Hear the victory sound.
Don't be dazzled
by the flashing lights.
You deserve them.

Press **QUESTRON**
on the triangle.

The red light and sound
say "Try again." Lift
QUESTRON off the page and
wait for the sound to stop.

Count Down

Press **Questron** on the box in the picture which matches the number at the beginning of each row.

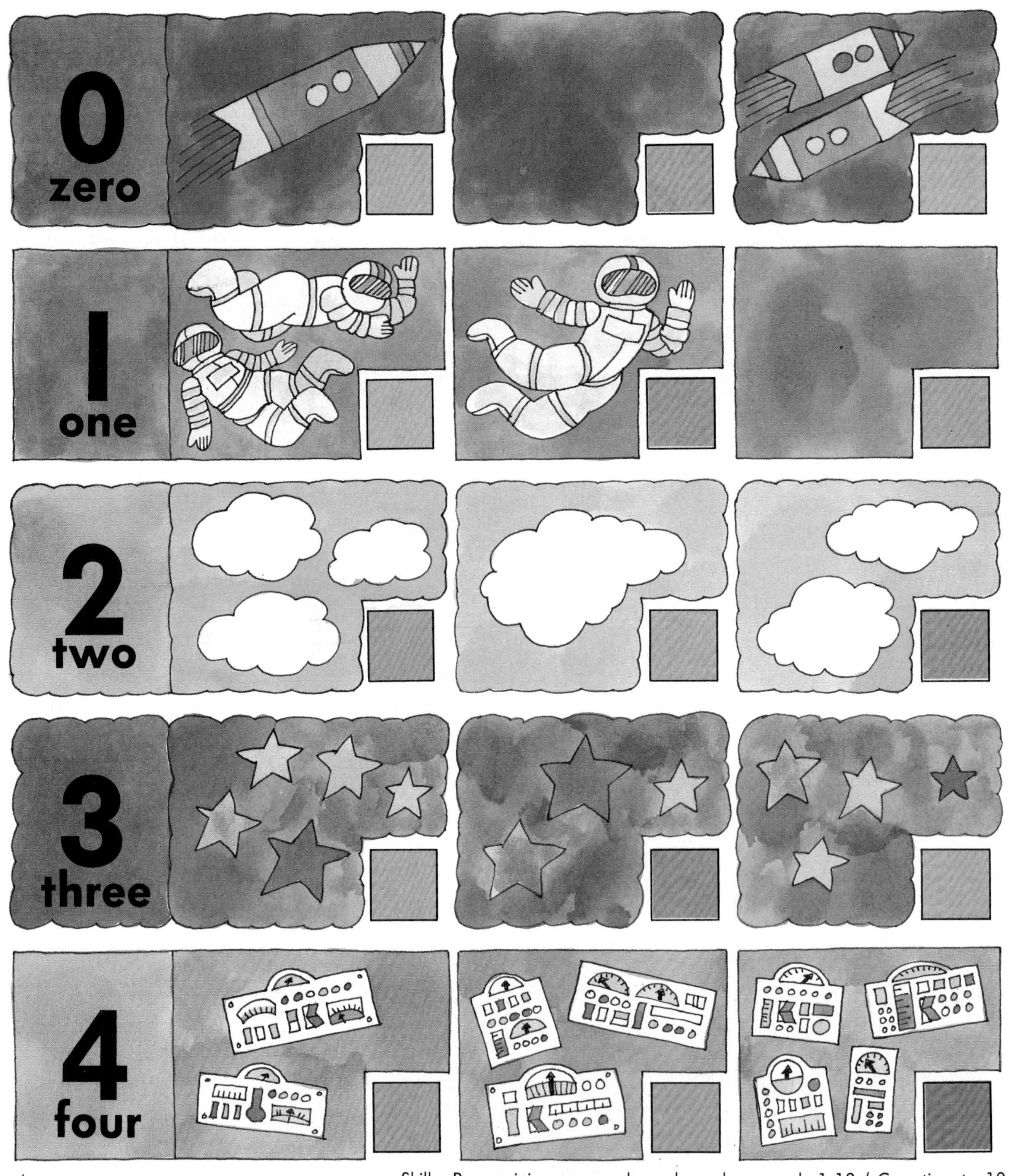

Skills: Recognizing numerals and number words 1-10 / Counting to 10

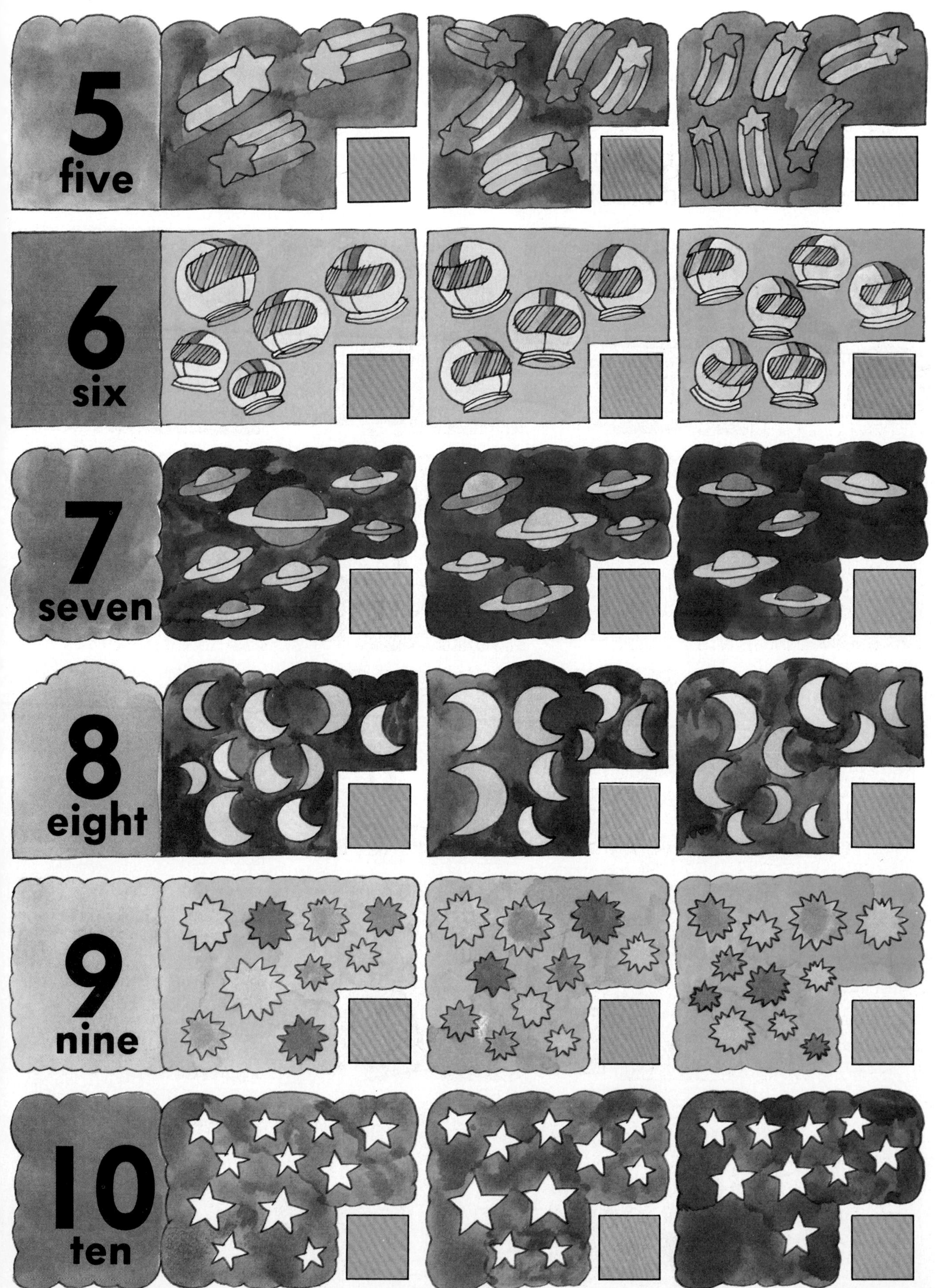
5
five
6
six
7
seven
8
eight
9
nine
10
ten

In All Kinds of Weather

Press **Questron** on the box in the picture which matches the number at the beginning of each row.

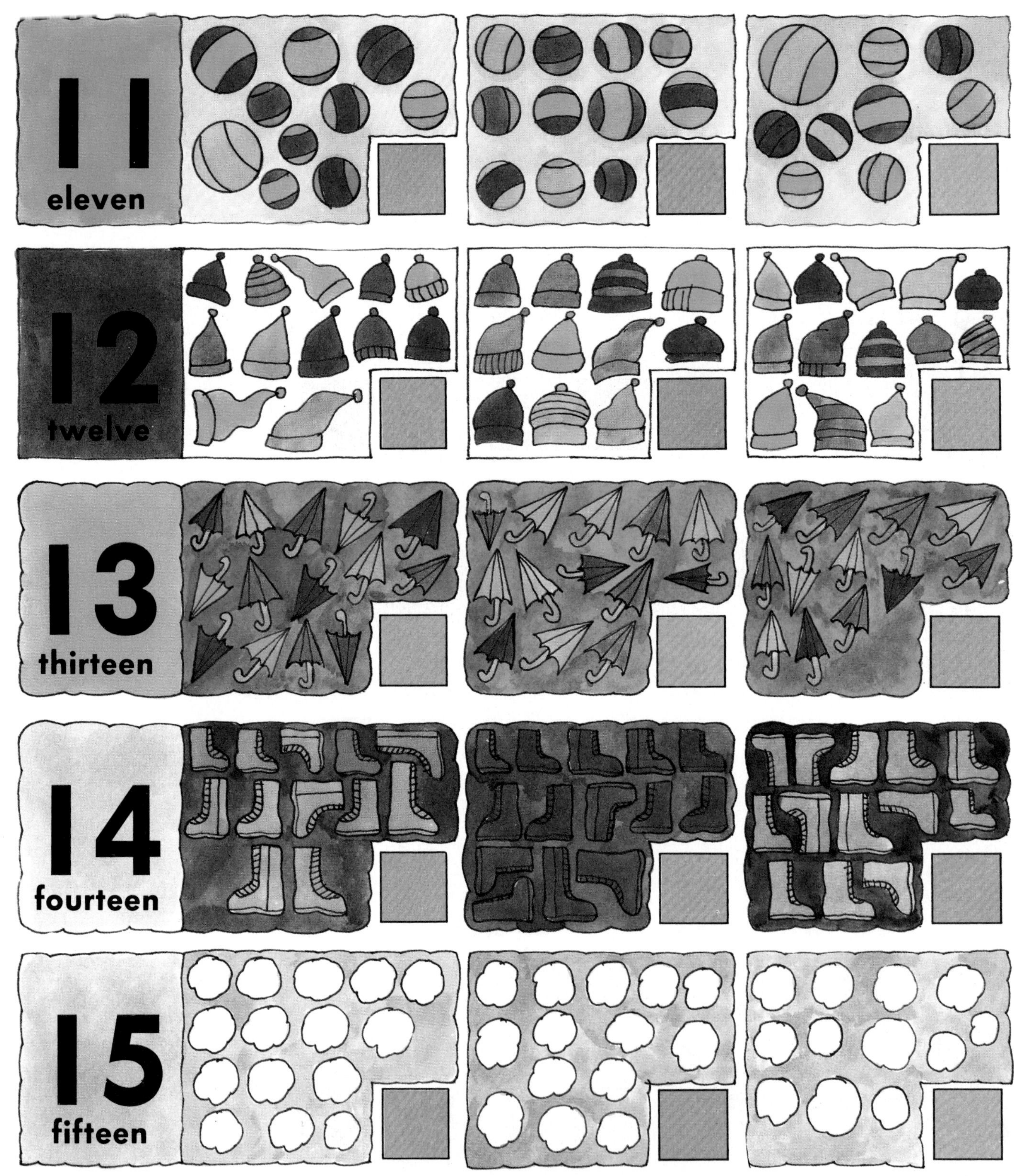

Skills: Recognizing numerals and number words 11-20 / Counting 11 to 20

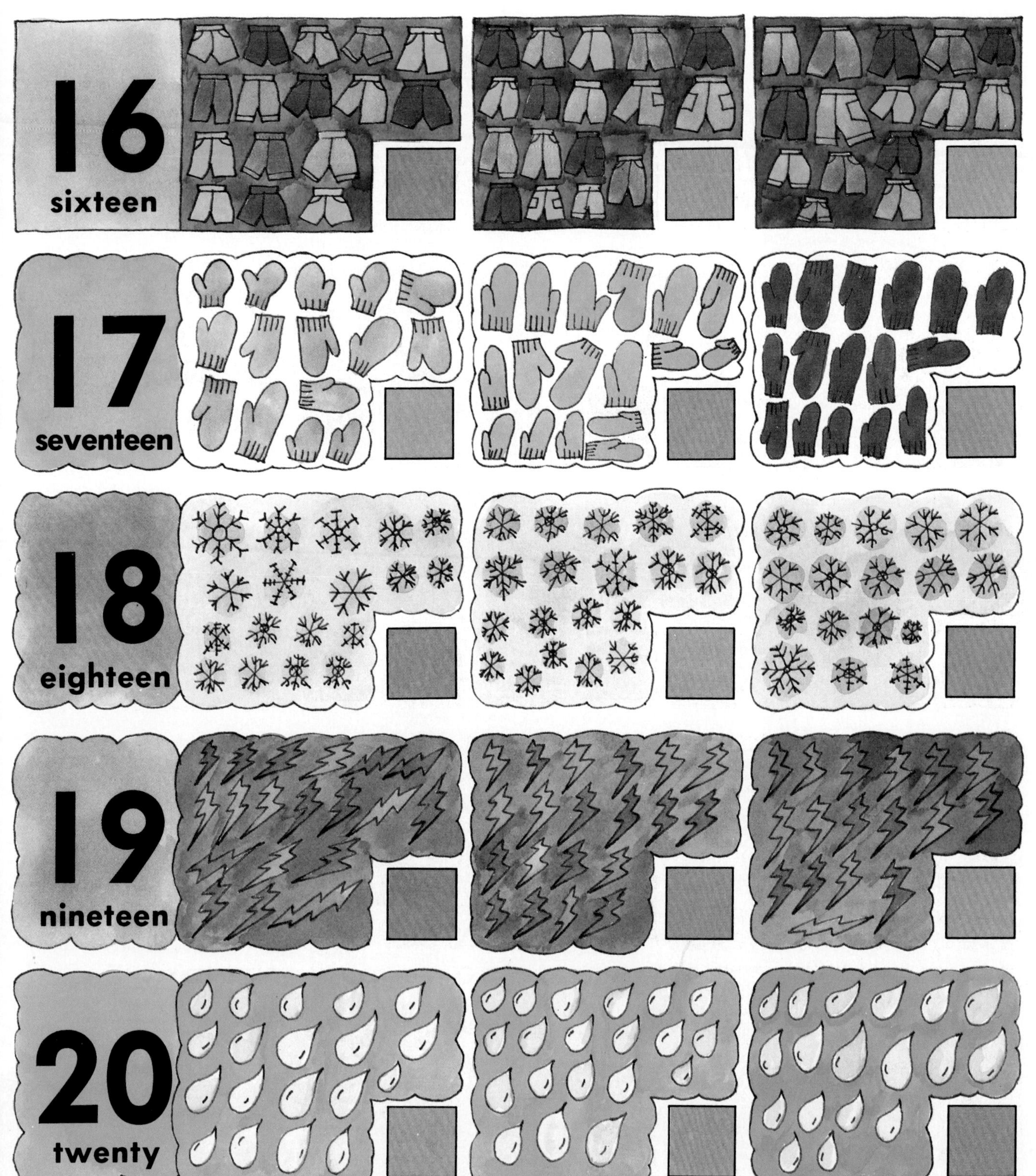
16
sixteen
17
seventeen
18
eighteen
19
nineteen
20
twenty

In the Swim

Solve each puzzle. If the total is **3**, press **Questron** on the box.

3

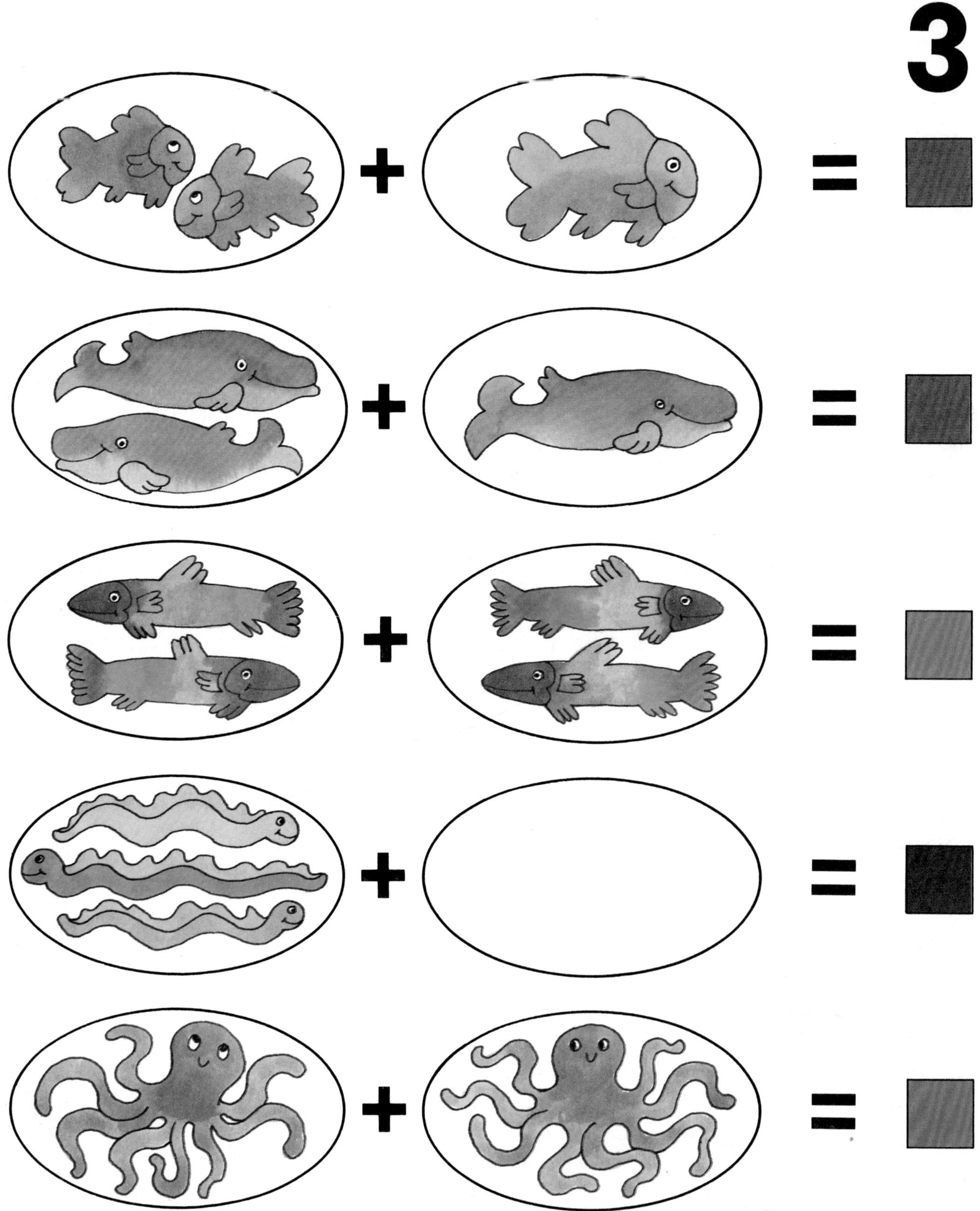

Skill: Recognizing sets that total 3

For the Birds

Solve each puzzle. If the total is **4**, press **Questron** on the box.

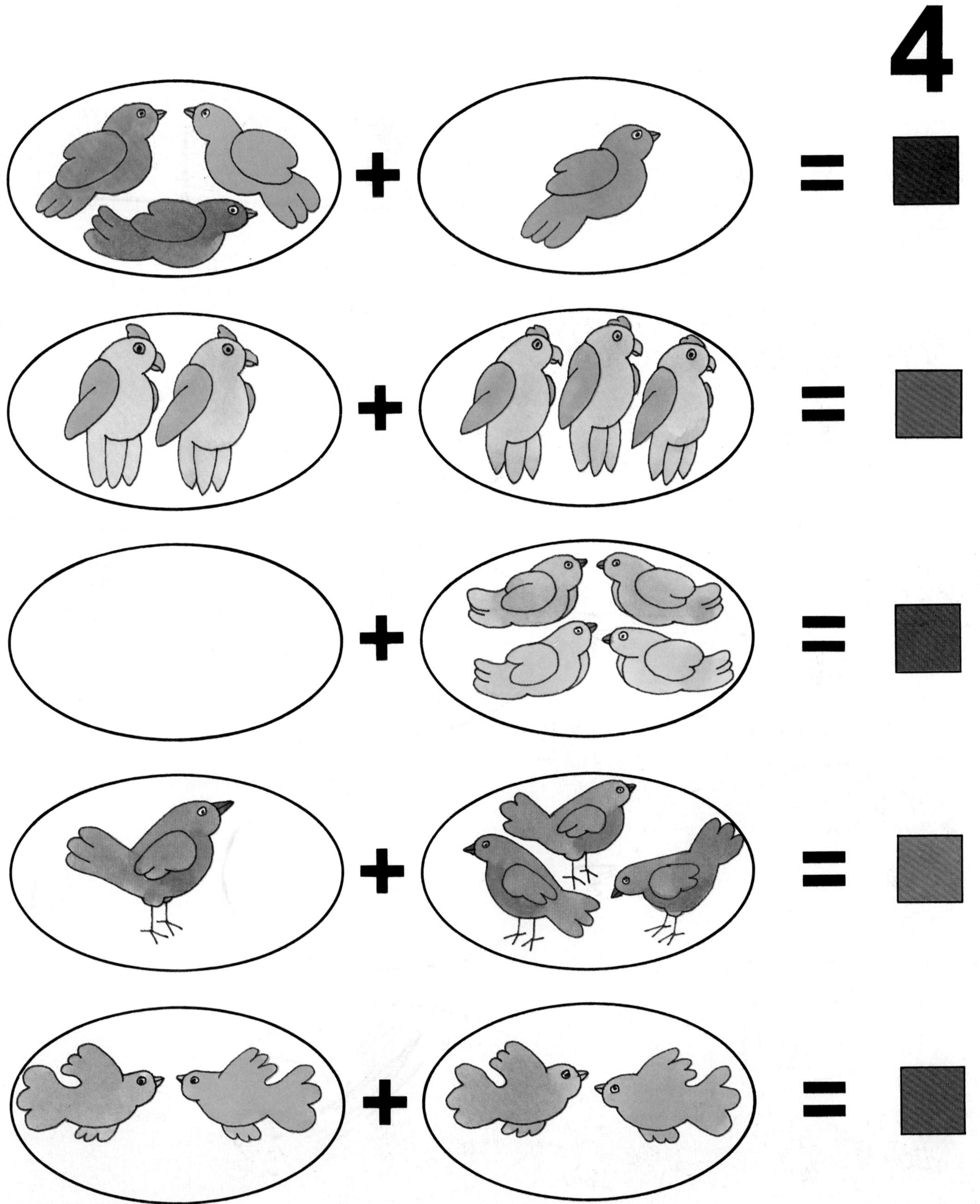

Skill: Recognizing sets that total 4

Party Time

Solve each puzzle. If the total is **5**, track **Questron** to the number **5**. Start on the ★.

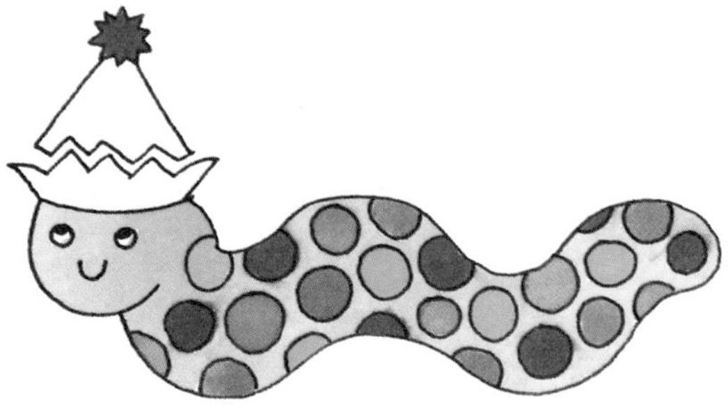

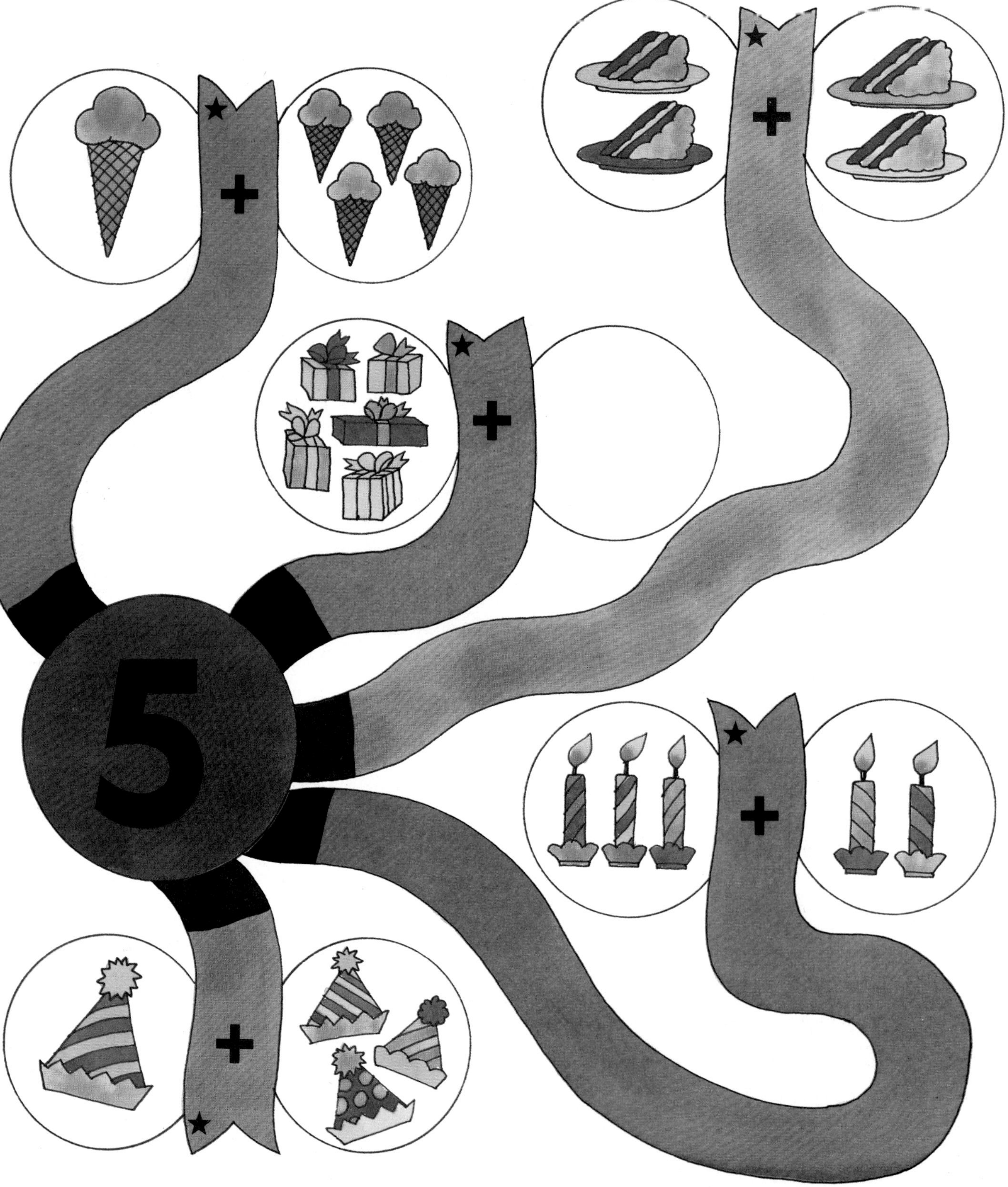

★ +

★ +

★ +

★ +

★ +

5

In the Farmyard

Solve each puzzle. If the total is **6**, track **Questron** to the number **6**. Start on the ★.

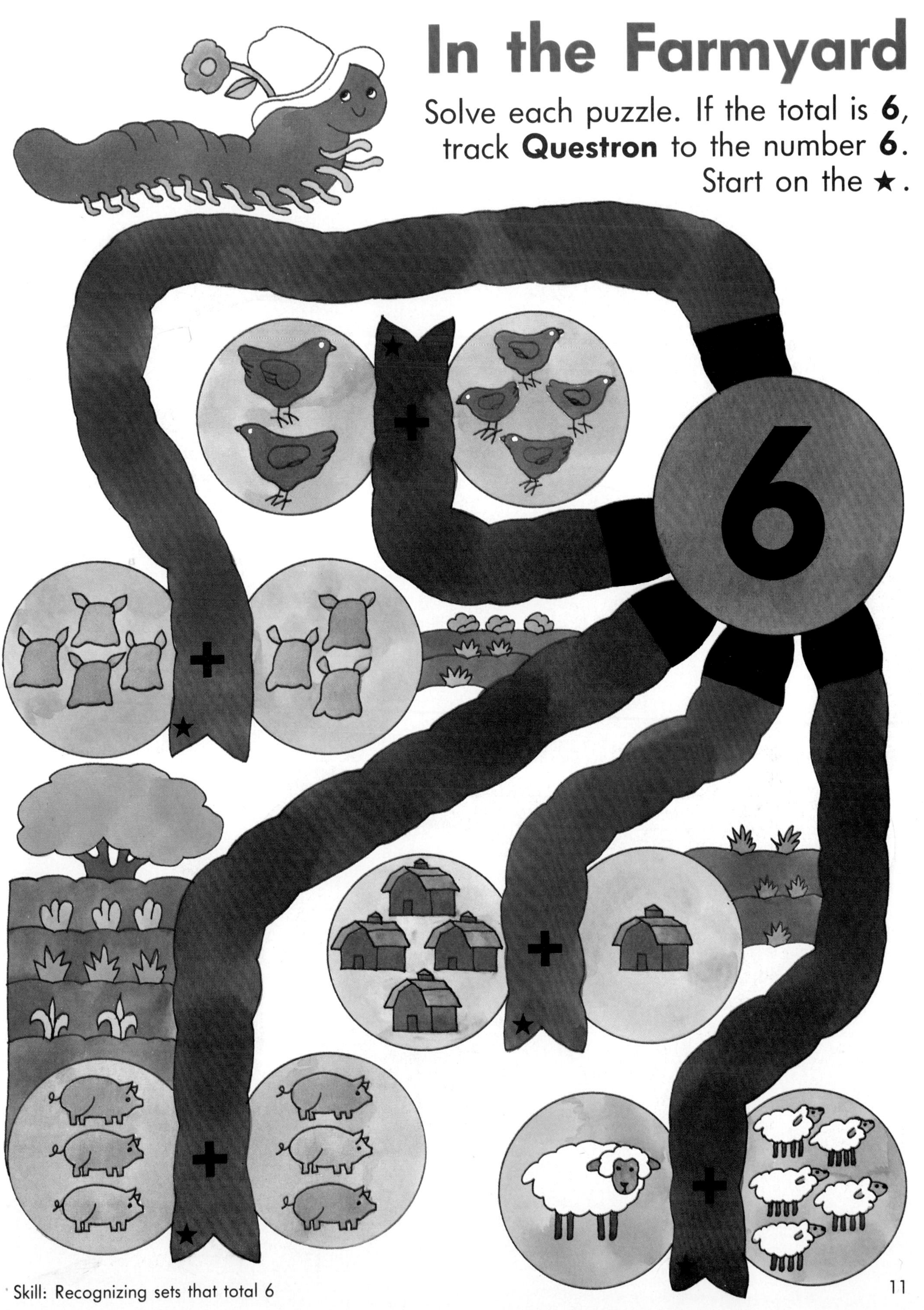

Pet Parade

Press **Questron** on the correct answer box.

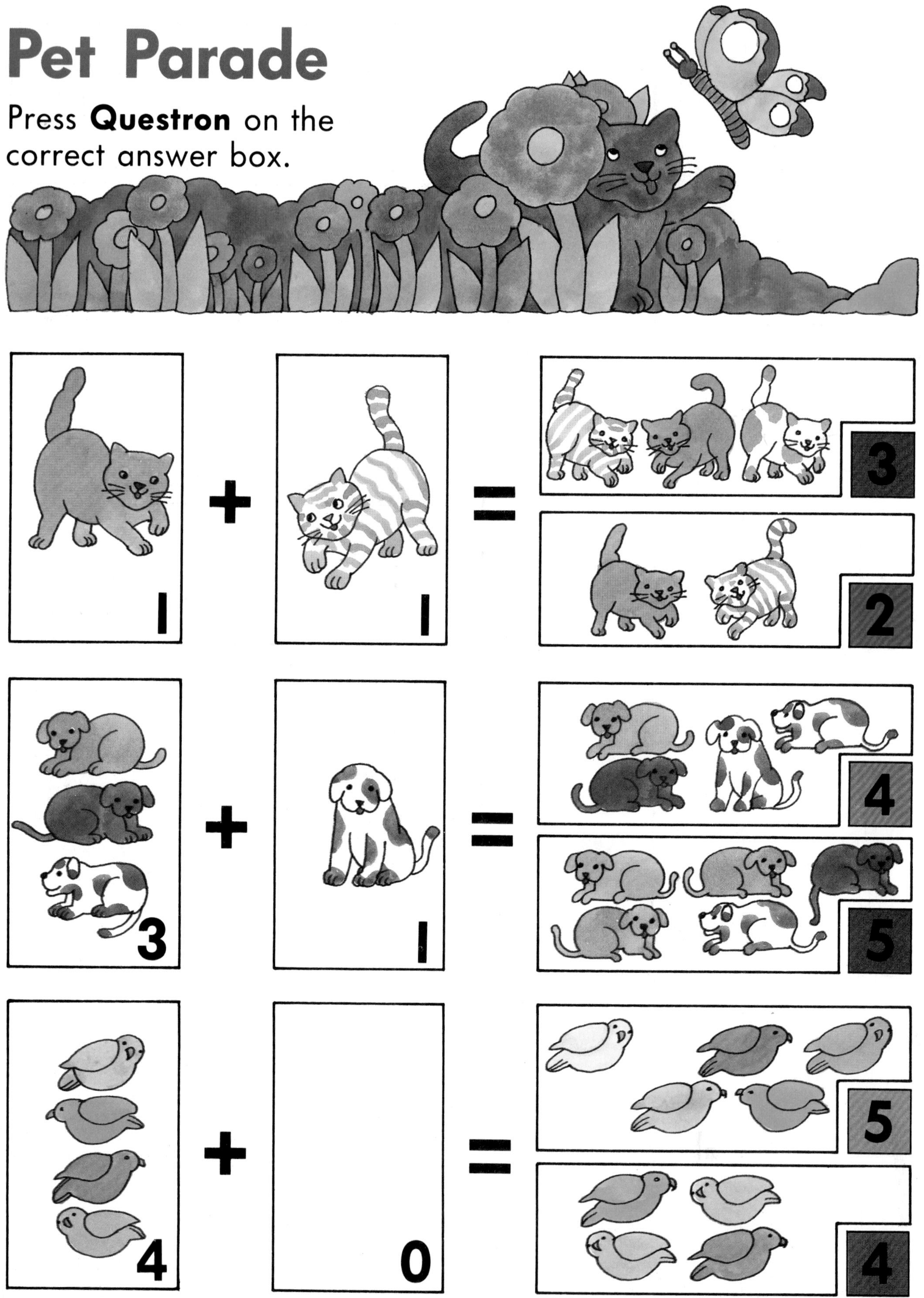

Skill: Completing number sentences

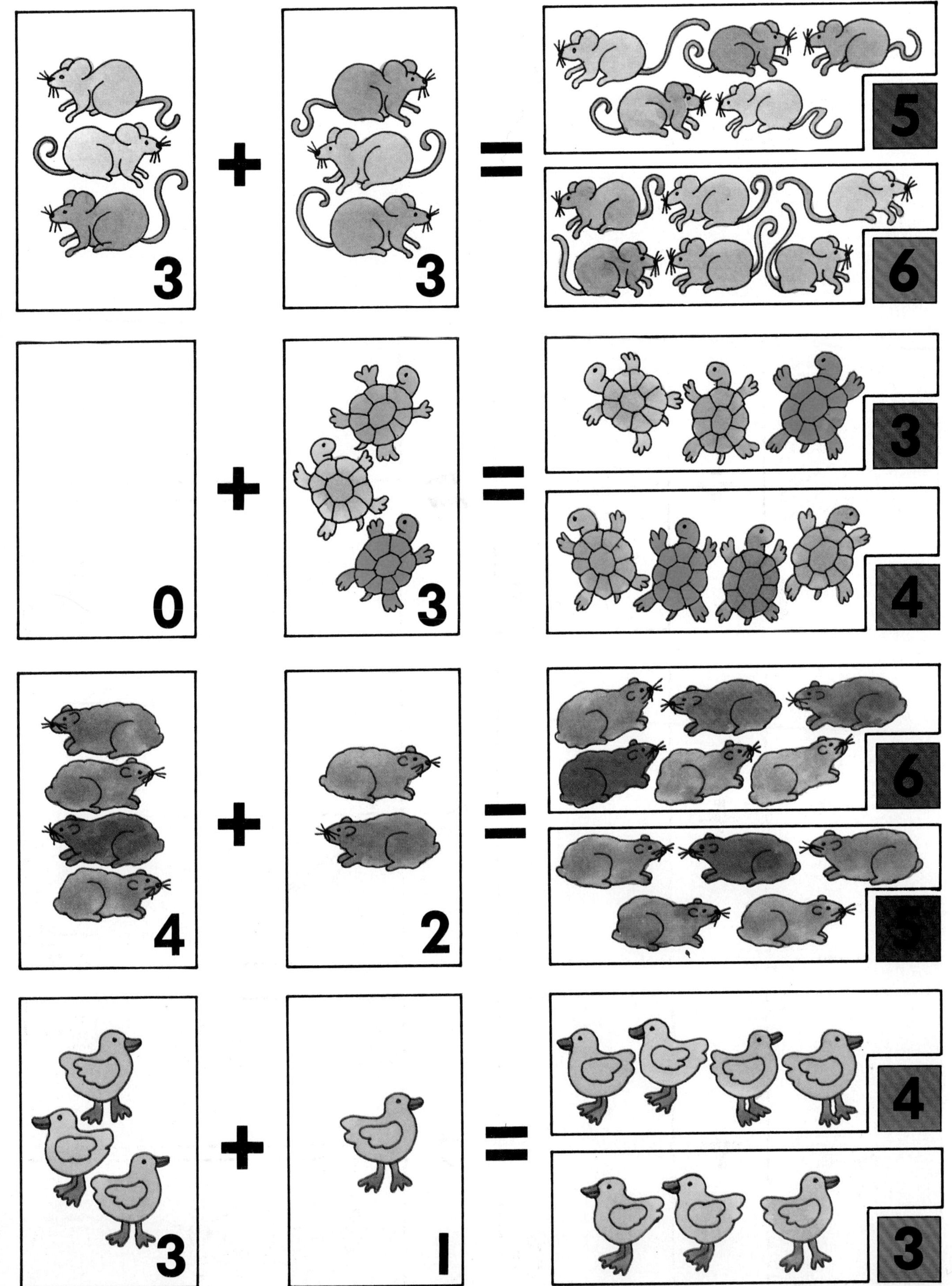

3
3
5
6
0
3
3
4
4
2
6
5
3
1
4
3

A Day in the Park

Press **Questron** on the correct answer.

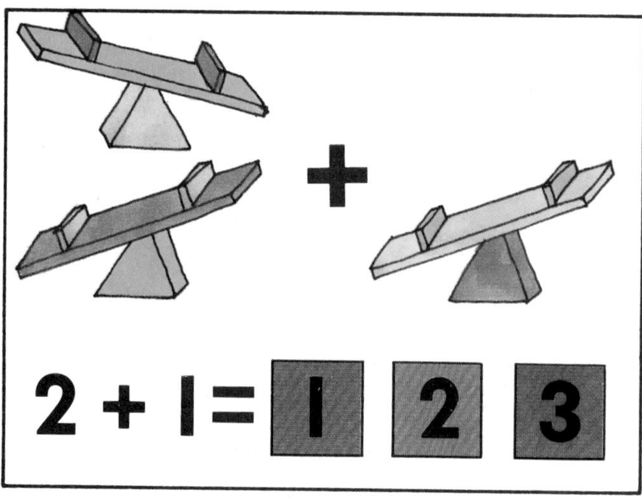

2 + 1 = 1 2 3

1 + 1 = 1 2 3

3 + 3 = 4 5 6

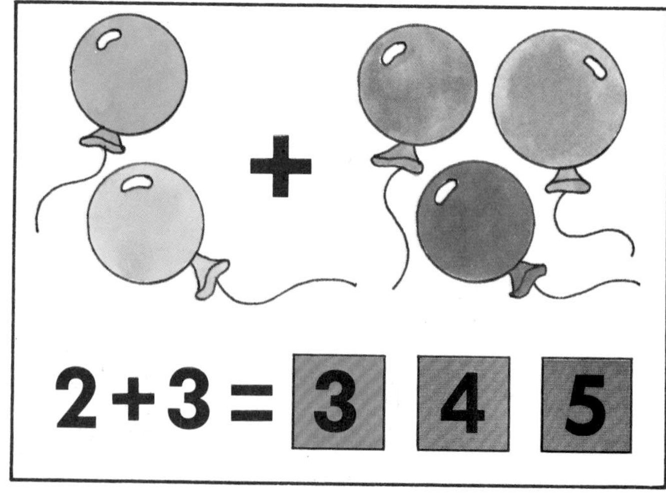

2 + 3 = 3 4 5

Skill: Completing number sentences

2 + 3 = 4 5 6

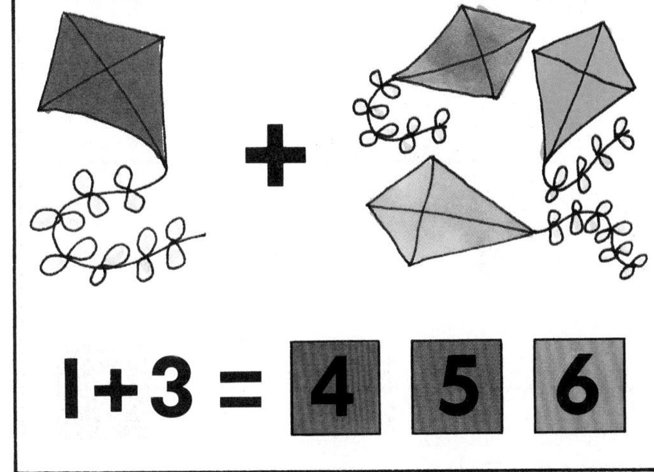

1 + 3 = 4 5 6

5 + 1 = 4 5 6

1 + 1 = 0 1 2

Rodeo Ride

Track **Questron** on the path that has the correct answers. Start on the ★.

Skill: Identifying correct number sentences

4 + 1
3
Stop
5
5
2 + 2
4
2
1+1
3
5
4+2
6

Numbers on Ice

Track **Questron** on the correct path. Start on the ★.

Skills: Counting by twos / Recognizing even and odd numbers

Taste Treats

Find the totals in the picture at the top of the page. Press **Questron** on the correct answer.

How many in the big picture?

How many in the big picture?

How many  in the big picture?

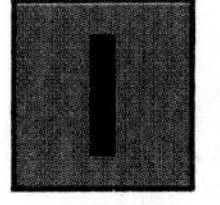

How many in the big picture?

How many in the big picture?

How many  in the big picture?

Skill: Adding items of the same kind

Flying High

Solve each puzzle. If the total is **7**, press **Questron** on the box.

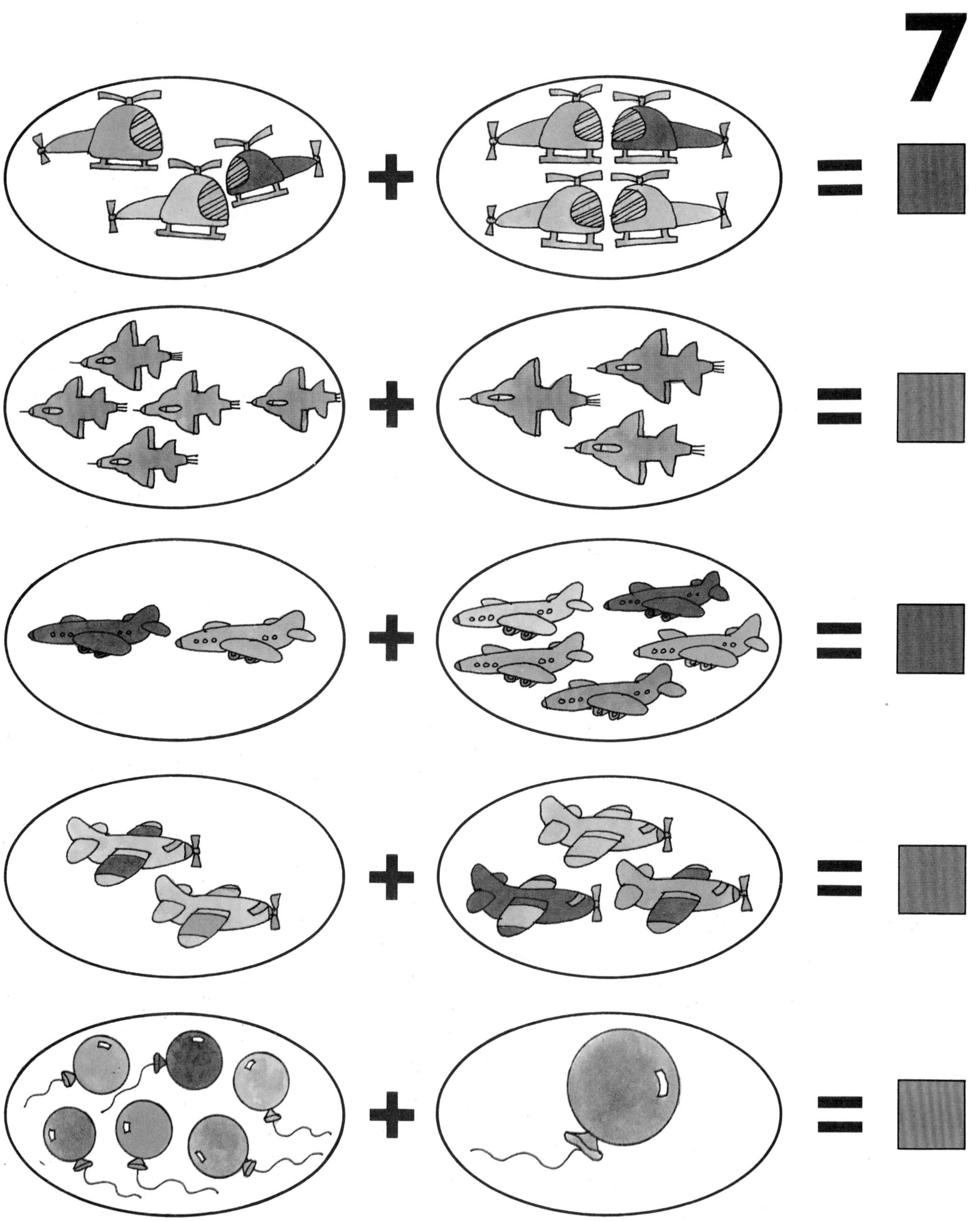

Through the Magic of Electronics

THE QUESTRON™ SYSTEM

Transforms Learning into Fun

Congratulations! You are the owner of a unique, new teaching product that turns the fun of games into the joy of learning. QUESTRON combines the latest electronic technology with beautifully illustrated full-color books.

QUESTRON Electronic Books are available for all ages and will provide endless hours of challenging entertainment. Correct answers are determined immediately, and QUESTRON Electronic Books can be used over and over.

QUESTRON itself is a unique electronic device that contains a magic microchip which "senses" correct or incorrect answers and signals the user with "right" or "wrong" sounds and lights. In addition, it provides a "victory" sound and flashing light pattern when certain sets of questions or games are completed. QUESTRON, powered by a nine-volt battery, should have an especially long life, since it is activated only when an answer is being sought. QUESTRON Electronic Books are on sale wherever the QUESTRON Wand is sold.

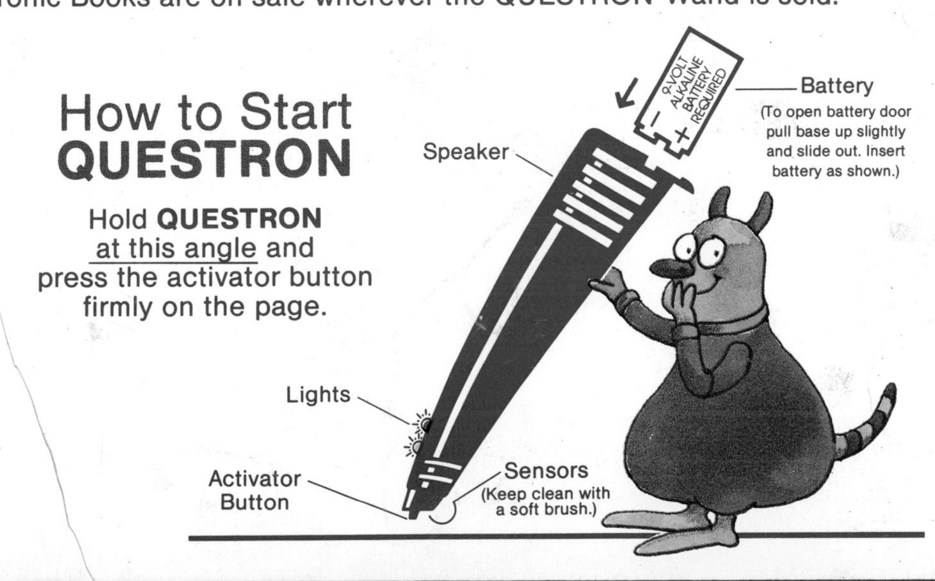

How to Use **QUESTRON**

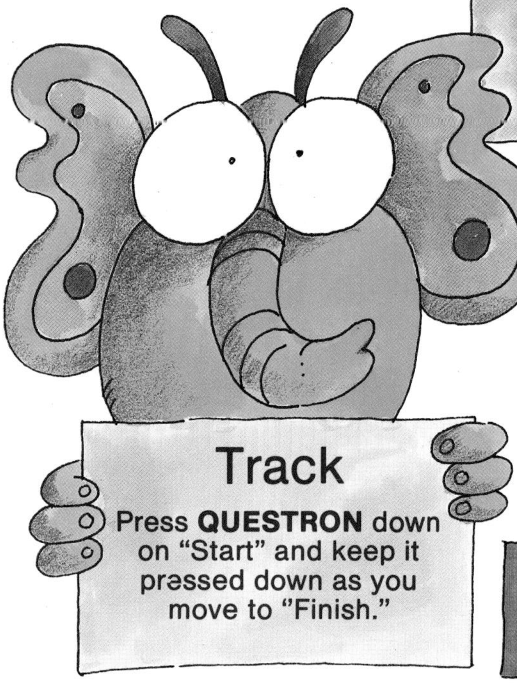
Track
Press **QUESTRON** down on "Start" and keep it pressed down as you move to "Finish."

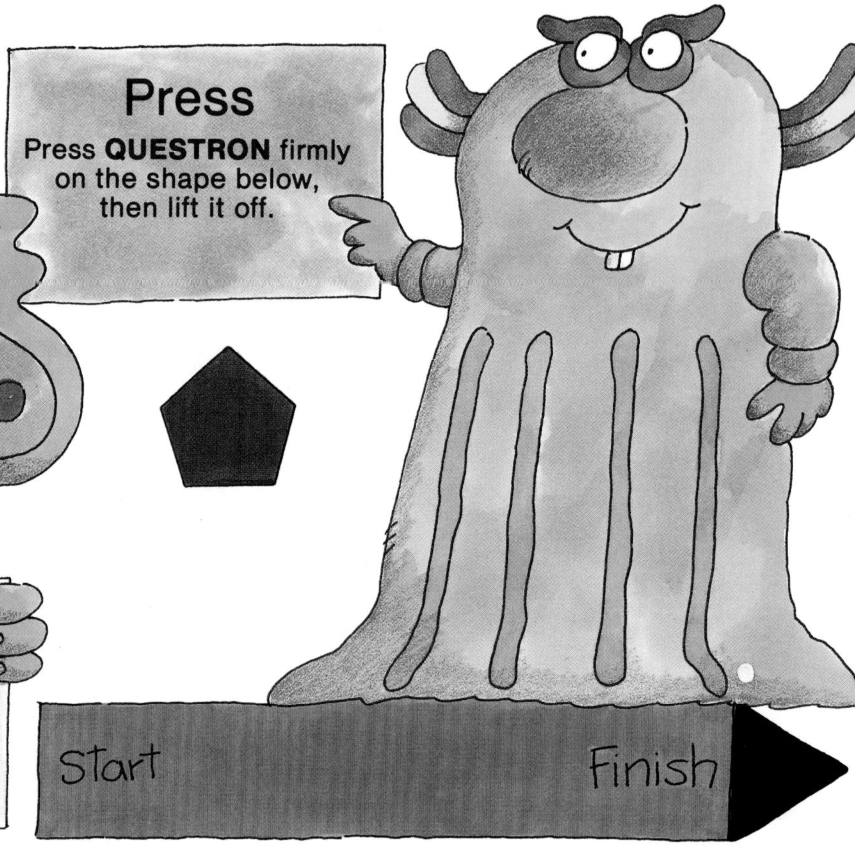
Press
Press **QUESTRON** firmly on the shape below, then lift it off.
Start
Finish

Right and Wrong with **QUESTRON**

Press **QUESTRON** on the square.

Press **QUESTRON** on the circle.

Press **QUESTRON** on the triangle.

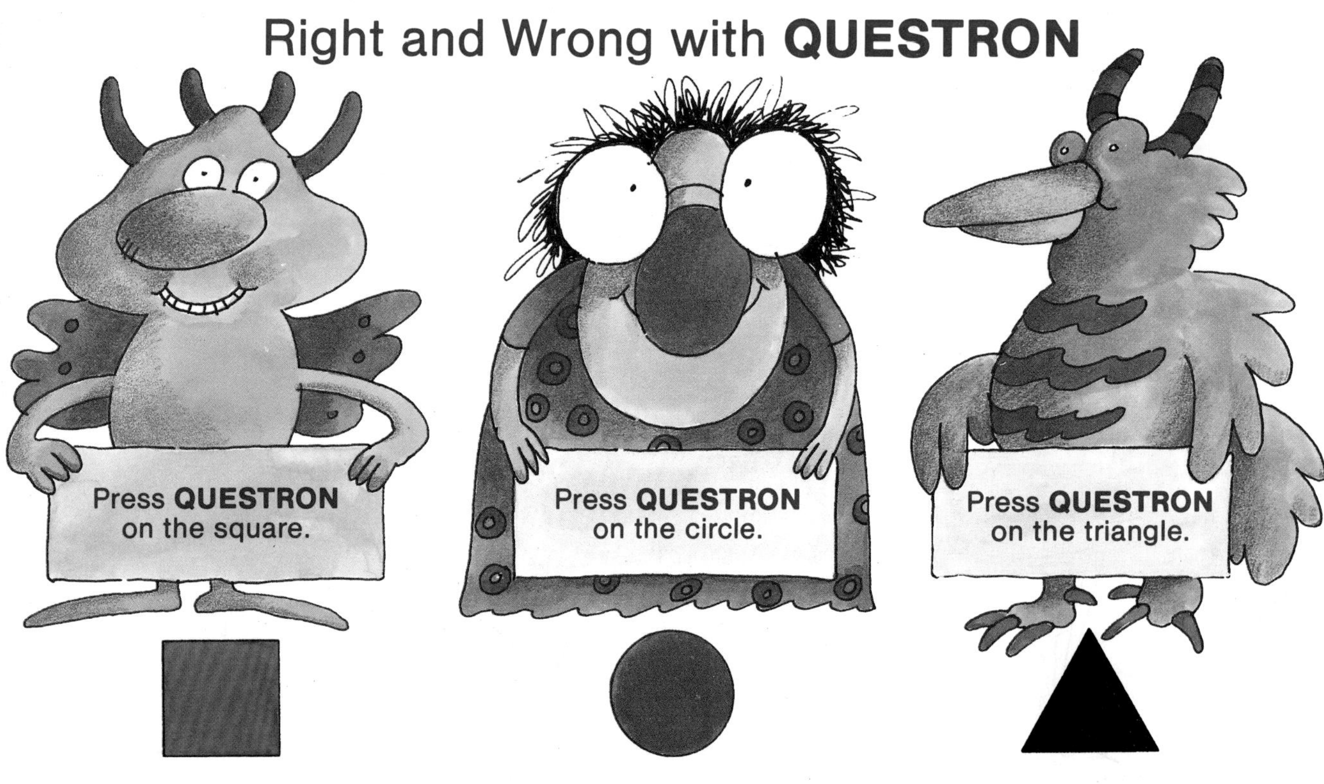

See the green light flash. Hear the sound. This green light and sound say "You are correct."

The red light and sound say "Try again." Lift **QUESTRON** off the page and wait for the sound to stop.

Hear the victory sound. Don't be dazzled by the flashing lights. You deserve them.

How many? Press **QUESTRON** on each correct answer.

What starts with "p"? Press **QUESTRON** on each picture that starts with "p".

Questron Trivia

Press **QUESTRON** on the colored square next to the correct answer.

What was the lowest land temperature ever recorded?

−106°F 

−127°F

−115°F

−148°F 

The largest known jellyfish is called the Lion's Mane. How many poisonous tentacles does it have?

8,800

4,300 

1,200 

6,900 

In astrology, what name is given to the sign of the bull?

Leo 

Taurus 

Scorpio

Capricorn 

In what game does each player use a racquet but not a ball?

Squash 

Badminton 

Lacrosse 

Tennis 

Please note that when your Questron's 9-volt alkaline battery needs replacing, Questron will begin to malfunction; it may always sound "right," it may always sound "wrong," or the sound levels will change.

Published by Price/Stern/Sloan Publishers, Inc., 410 North La Cienega Boulevard, Los Angeles, California 90048. Distributed by Random House, Inc., 201 East 50th Street, New York, New York 10022

ISBN: 0-394-87684-9

Patents Pending. Printed in Hong Kong.

PRICE/STERN/SLOAN – RANDOM HOUSE, INC.

Publishers, Inc., Los Angeles *New York*

Circus Time

Solve each puzzle. If the total is **8**, press **Questron** on the box.

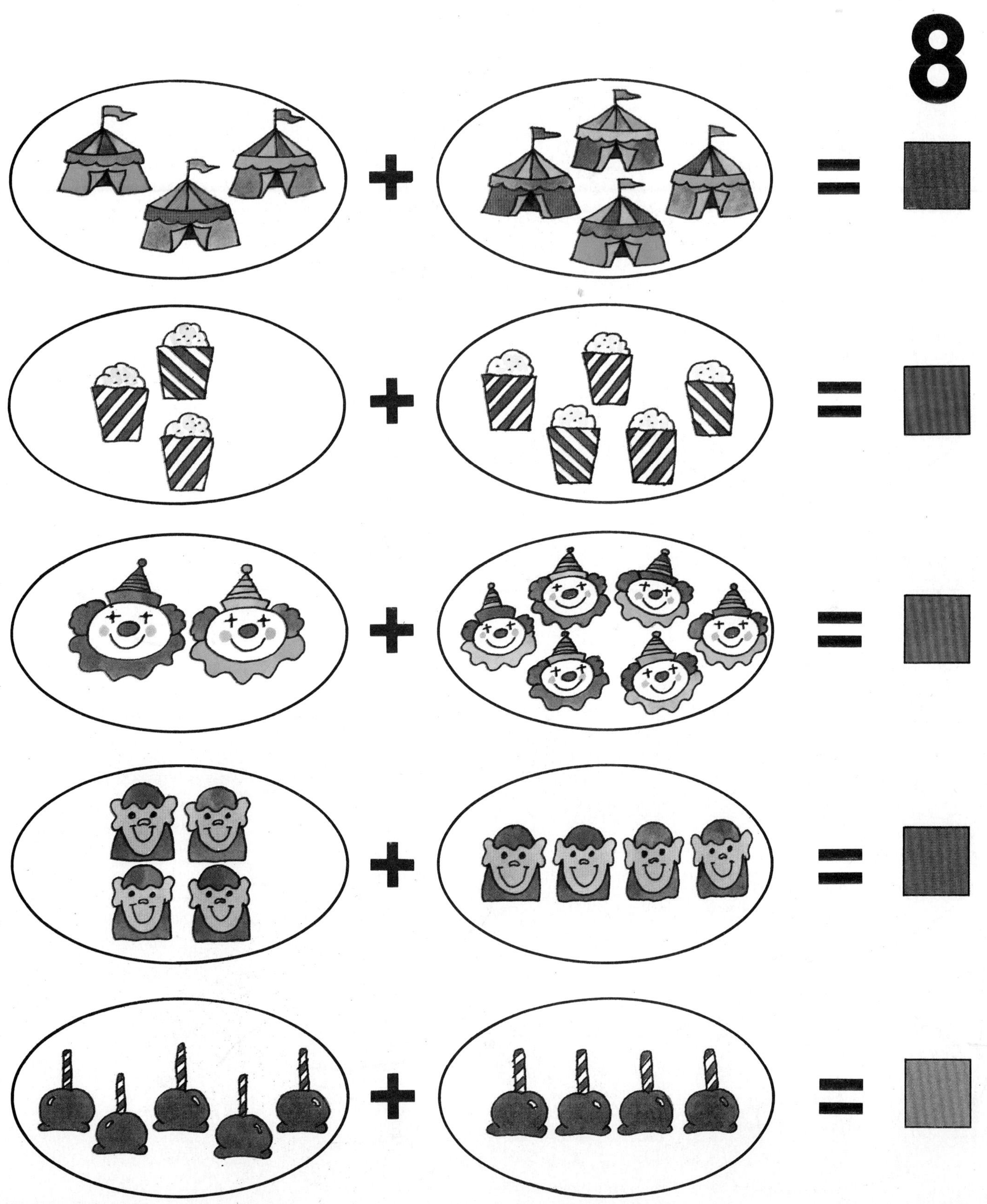

Winter Fun

Solve each puzzle. If the total is **9**, track **Questron** to the number **9**. Start on the ★.

Skill: Recognizing sets that total 9

Artists at Work

Solve each puzzle. If the total is **10**, track **Questron** to the number **10**. Start on the ★.

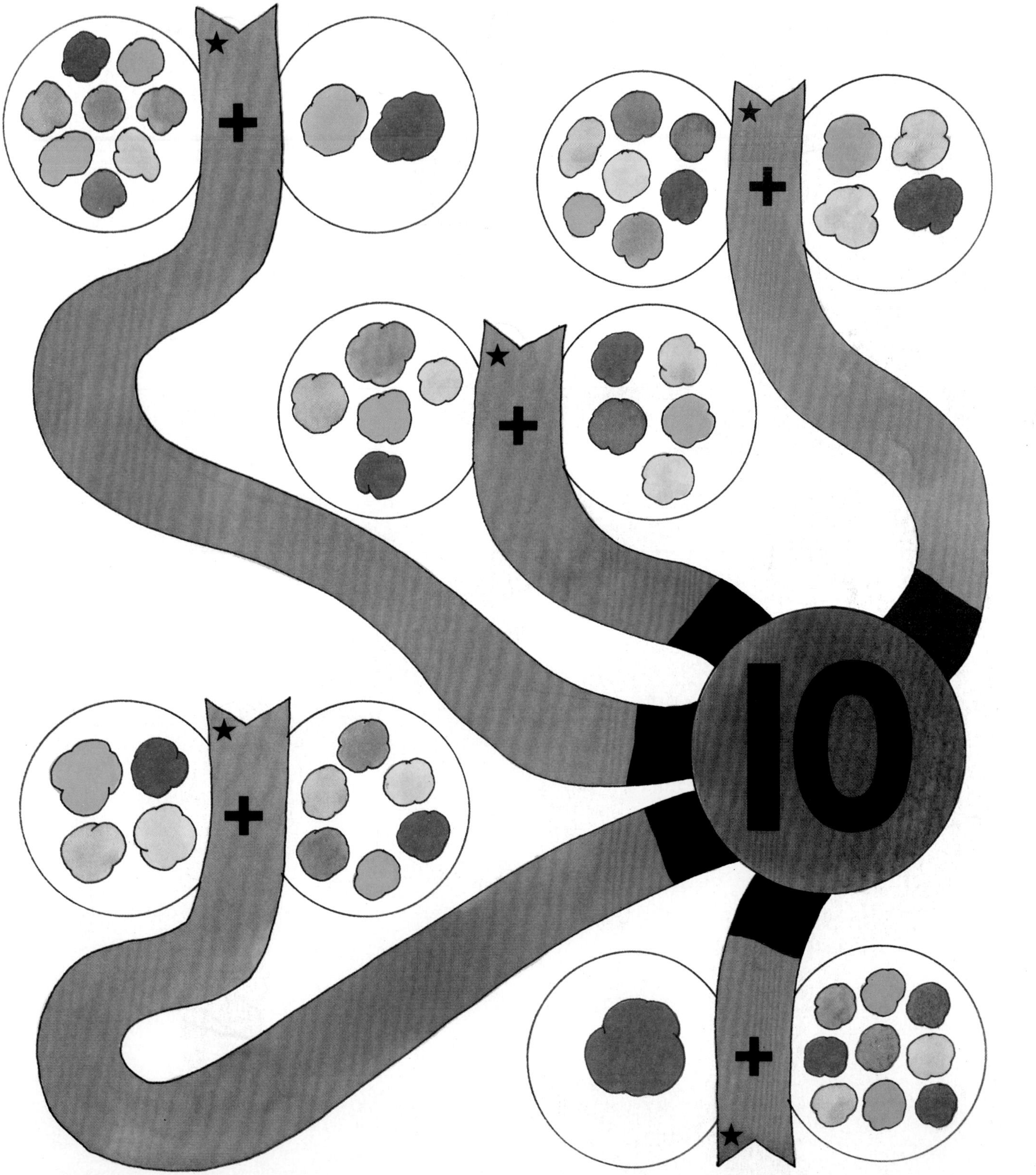

★ +

★ +

★ +

★ +

★ +

10

A Sporting Chance

Press **Questron** on the correct answers.

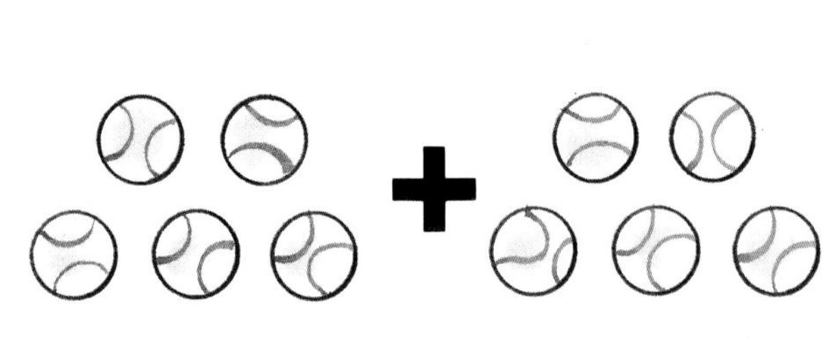

5 + 5 = 8 9 10

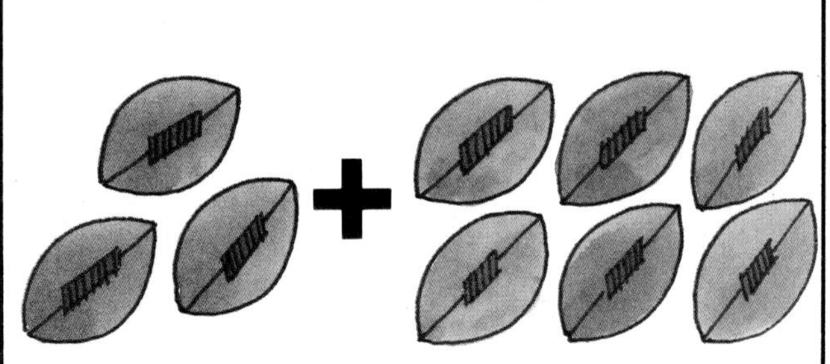

3 + 6 = 7 8 9

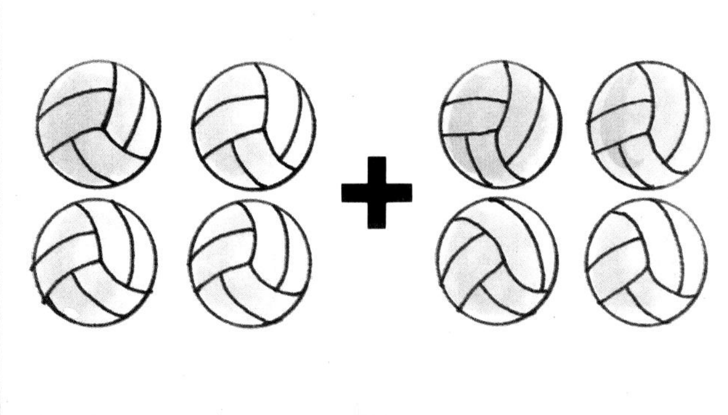

4 + 4 = 6  

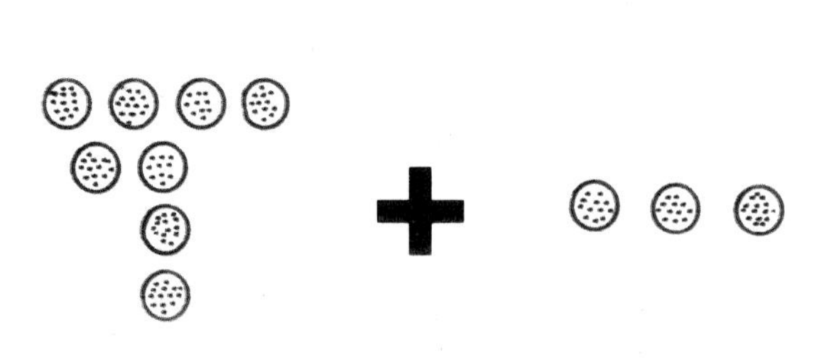

8 + 3 =   

Skill: Solving addition problems

5 + 3 = 8 9 10

3 + 4 = 7 8 9

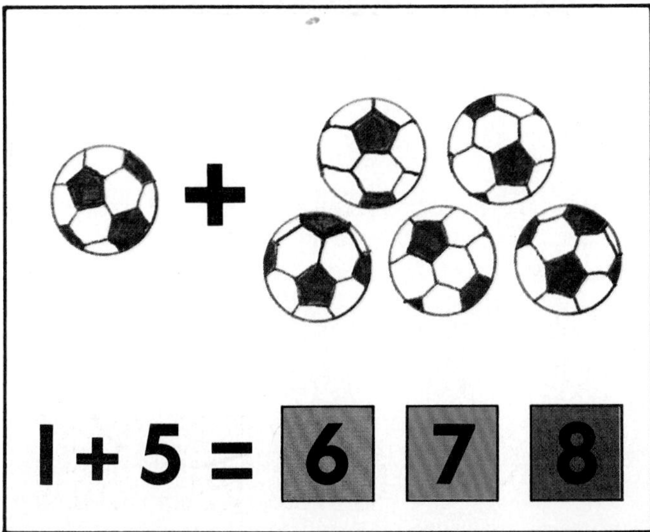

1 + 5 = 6 7 8

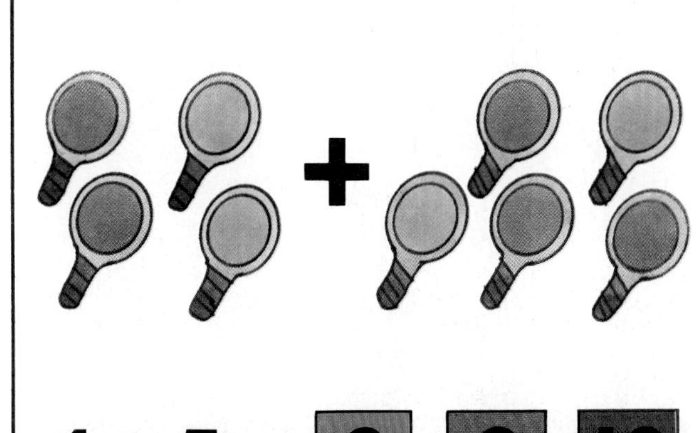

4 + 5 = 8 9 10

Juggling Numbers

Press **Questron** on the correct answer to each clown's puzzle.

Skill: Solving addition problems

7
6
5
4
+2
9
8
10
1
+9
8
10
9
5
+3
9
8
7
4
+5
Touch my hat
when you solve
all the puzzles
correctly.

Loading Up

Look at the number on each truck. Only the containers with that total belong on the truck. Press **Questron** on the containers that belong.

Skill: Identifying addition problems with given sums

9
4
+5
8
+2
6
+3
1
+8
5
5
+0
3
+3
4
+1
3
+2
8
6
+3
4
+4
7
+1
5
+3
3
3
+0
2
+1
1
+3
1
+1

On Safari

Press **Questron** on the correct answers.

3  are in the tree.

2 more  climb up.

How many in all?

5 go to the river.

4 more  go.

How many in all?

.

Sally has 2 more .

How many in all?

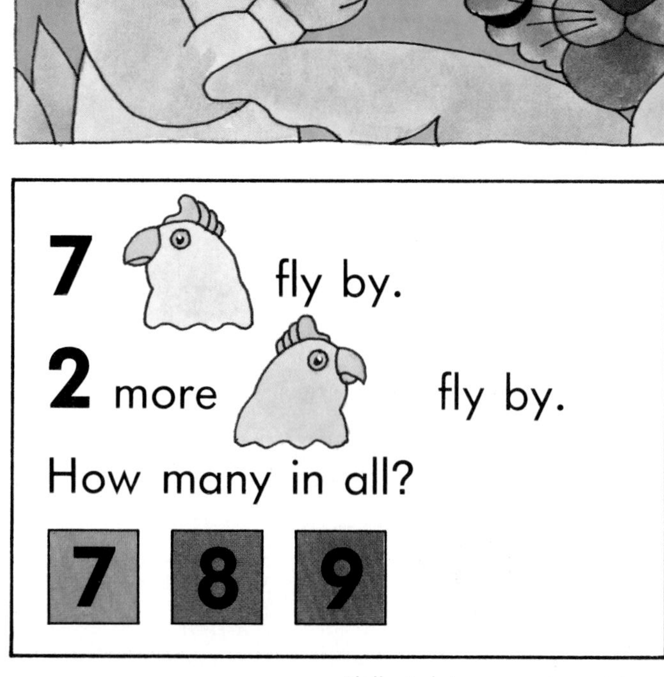

7 fly by.

2 more fly by.

How many in all?

7 8 9

Skill: Solving word problems

I see 6 .

Joe sees 4 more.

How many in all?

8 9 10

4 go by.

2 more go by.

How many in all?

4 5 6

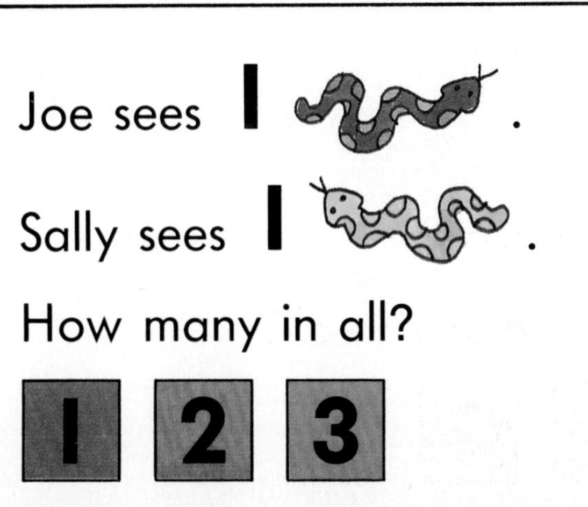

Joe sees 1 .

Sally sees 1 .

How many in all?

1 2 3

3 roar.

1 roars.

How many in all?

3 4 5

THE QUESTRON LIBRARY OF ELECTRONIC BOOKS

A series of books specially designed to reach—and teach—and entertain children of all ages

QUESTRON ELECTRONIC WORKBOOKS

Early Childhood

My First Counting Book
My First ABC Book
My First Book of Animals
Shapes and Sizes
Preschool Skills
My First Vocabulary
My First Nursery Rhymes
Autos, Ships, Trains and Planes
Reading Readiness
My First Words
My First Numbers
Going Places
Kindergarten Skills

Grades 1–5

My First Reading Book (K–1)
First Grade Skills (1)
My First Book of Addition (1–2)
My First Book of Multiplication (2–3)
I Want to Be... (2–5)
Number Fun (2–5)
Word Fun (2–5)

ELECTRONIC QUIZBOOKS FOR THE WHOLE FAMILY

Trivia Fun and Games
How, Why, Where and When
More How, Why, Where and When
World Records and Amazing Facts

PRICE/STERN/SLOAN Publishers, Inc., Los Angeles – RANDOM HOUSE, INC. New York